The Stolen Sun

A Story of Native Alaska

Amanda Hall

Eerdmans Books for Young Readers
Grand Rapids, Michigan • Cambridge, U.K.

For Lisa, plentifully, also for Ben and Melissa — A.H

*The themes in this story form an important part of
Native Alaskan belief and culture.*

This edition published in 2002 under license from Frances Lincoln Limited by
Eerdmans Books for Young Readers
An imprint of Wm. B. Eerdmans Publishing Co.
255 Jefferson Ave. S.E., Grand Rapids, Michigan 49503
P.O. Box 163, Cambridge CB3 9PU U.K.

Printed in Singapore

02 03 04 05 06 07 08   7 6 5 4 3 2 1

Hall, Amanda.
The stolen sun / written by Amanda Hall. p. cm.
ISBN 0-8028-5225-4 (cloth : alk. paper)
1. Inuit—Folklore. 2. Raven (Legendary character)—Legends. I. Title.
E99.E7 H2198 2002
398.2'089'9712—dc21
2001023969

www.eerdmans.com/youngreaders

*O*nce upon a time, before ice and before snow, the sky arched like a giant tent over the top of the world. Higher still, in a land above the sky, lived Raven.

In those days there was a hole in the sky linking our world with Raven's. One day Raven flew down through the hole to see what lay below.

To his delight he found mountains, rivers, and forests
on which the sun shone brightly. But there were no creatures.
So Raven created animals and people, birds, and fish.
He gave a special song to the people to remind them to
love and respect the life around them.

As time passed, the people living on the earth became discontented.
They began to mutter and argue and shout and rage,
until Raven's song was no more than a whisper among them.

Raven watched and saw greed and violence spread like a shadow across the land, and he grew angry.

With a great shriek, Raven tore the shining sun from its place in the sky. Back he flew through the hole in the sky with the sun tucked under his wing. He hid the sun in a secret place, leaving the land below to freeze in the silver light of the moon.

Raven vowed never to return to earth. Plucking one small farewell feather from his breast, he left it to float on the wind as he flew away.

Who knows how long the tiny feather drifted in the cold dark air?

Down, down, down it floated until it landed on an icy stream.

One cold morning, a woman went to fetch water. She lifted the ladle to her lips and did not see the small black feather floating in the water as she drank.

That night she dreamed of dark fluttering wings, and Raven's forgotten song echoed through her dream.

In time the woman gave birth to a baby boy. He was as silent and beautiful as night itself, and she named him Little Darkness.

As she rocked him in her arms, she sang him her dream. The tiny baby listened intently, gazing up at her with his dark, dark eyes.

Little Darkness grew to be a fine, brave boy. Although he laughed and played

like other children, his mother sensed that he was somehow different.

One day Little Darkness went to the ice to fish and saw a dark shape nearby. It was a curious mask shaped like a bird's head. As Little Darkness touched it, a long-forgotten song breathed across the ice, making the surface shimmer and shimmer. Little Darkness lifted the mask over his head.

As he pulled the mask over his face, a great sound filled the sky.
Little Darkness felt himself full of power. His shoulders began to ache.
Something was growing on his back. He had wings!

Then he was flying up and up, following the song that called him.

Higher and higher went the song and the winged boy, until they came to the hole in the sky. The song floated through, but when Little Darkness tried to follow a terrible screeching came from up above. It was Raven whirling down, trying to catch the intruder.

Little Darkness held up his hands to shield his face. Gasping, he pulled off the mask and saw a cloud of dark feathers swirling in front of him. He fell back, and as he fell his wings disappeared. Then all was blackness.

Slowly Little Darkness awoke. At first he thought he was in his mother's arms, for he felt her warmth and heard her lullaby. But no — he was floating through the air. Cradled by a gentle mist, he was carried up through the hole in the sky.

Above the sky he drifted, across strange valleys and seas,
until the mist set him down at the foot of a steep mountain.
It was made entirely of ice, and at its center a dim light glowed.

Little Darkness had never seen such light before. It looked warm and bright, and he wanted it. Taking his axe from his belt, he began to hack his way up the frozen mountainside towards the light.

While he hacked, Little Darkness sang. At first he sang in a small voice, but as he climbed his voice grew. The warmth of his song made the wall wet against his hands. Above him he could hear the screech of Raven, but still he did not stop.

Water began to stream down around him, threatening to wash away his foothold. Ice crashed down the mountainside, but he sang out even louder.

And as he sang, the glow from the mountain grew stronger. Now the icy walls were no more than a thin glassy veil. One more blow and the sun would be released. But just as Little Darkness raised his axe to strike, the last piece of ice broke away.

From up above, Raven saw his son falling.
No! He must not die! Down Raven swooped,
lifting Little Darkness to safety.

"Come," he commanded, and Little
Darkness climbed onto Raven's back.
He held on tightly to the short feathers around
Raven's neck, unafraid now of the fierce beak
and sharp claws.

Raven flew to the sun and grasped it
firmly. Off they flew, back over the seas and
valleys, back to the hole in the sky. Raven
dived down through it and cast the huge fiery
sphere up into the sky again, where it blazed
brightly, lighting up the whole world.

On the earth below, a mother gazed up
at the brilliant glittering sky. "Little Darkness!"
she cried. "You are safe! I can hear our song!
And the world will never live in darkness
again."